Fresh as a Daisy, Neat as a Pin

A Stepping-Stone Book

Fresh as a Daisy, Neat as a Pin

By WILLIAM WISE

Pictures by Dora Leder

Parents' Magazine Press • *New York*

Fresh as a Daisy, Neat as a Pin

Living creatures have many different ways
of keeping clean.

When a wild horse feels dirty, he lies on
his back in the grass. He begins to roll from
side to side. Each time he rolls in the grass
some of the dirt and dust come off his coat.

A house cat cleans herself by using her
tongue. She does this when her fur becomes
stuck together. After she has cleaned herself,
her fur is light and fluffy again. She looks
better, and feels better too.

Sometimes a whole family of animals
works together to keep clean. Monkeys do
this in the jungle. With their paws, they
pick dirt out of one another's fur.

A baby monkey is groomed this way too.
By watching his mother, the baby learns
how to use his own paws. Then, after he is
grown, he helps to keep the rest of the
family clean.

Some animals are not able to groom
themselves, though. The huge rhinoceros is
one of them. Insects called tics live on his
skin. The rhinoceros cannot reach the
insects with his feet, to rub them off. He
doesn't have paws to pick them off with,
either.

So the rhinoceros does a strange thing.
He lets a bird called the ox-pecker climb
around on his back. The ox-pecker picks off
the tics with his bill. Then he eats the tics.
In this way, the huge rhinoceros gets rid of
the insects that have been living on his skin.

There is a strange fish called the wrasse that lives in the warm seas. He always swims in the same place. When other fish have old skin that needs cleaning off, they swim over to the wrasse.

The wrasse picks off the old skin and eats it. After he has finished, the other fish swim away with their skins cleaned.

Many birds clean themselves by bathing.
In the country they have no trouble finding
water. They fly to the shores of lakes and
ponds. There they splash about, getting
the dirt out of their feathers.

Even in the city, birds like to bathe. But usually they have to wait till after it rains. Then the streets are filled with puddles of water. Fat pigeons walk in the puddles and clean themselves. Small sparrows hop in too, wetting their feathers and shaking the water out. While bathing, the sparrows make a great deal of noise. They seem happy to have found the chance to be clean again.

All kinds of living creatures try to keep themselves neat and well-groomed. This is true of people—as well as of horses and cats, fish and birds.

People like to bathe because they feel better after they've been in the water. People like to bathe, too, because they know that washing the dirt and sweat off their bodies helps to keep them healthy.

It has not always been easy, though, for people to keep clean. Many years ago, it was hard to get enough water for washing and bathing. When people *could* get enough water, they had no easy way to heat it. So, in many places, hardly anyone ever washed or took a bath. Sometimes people grew very dirty. That was one of the reasons why they often were sick.

The first man in the world to have a
bathtub may have been the king of an
island in the Mediterranean Sea, Crete.
The king lived in a fine palace. His palace
had a number of bathtubs with hot and cold
running water.

But the king of Crete lived more than
three thousand years ago. And from his day
to ours, many of the world's most famous
kings and queens took very few baths.

Two thousand years ago, the people of
Rome ruled much of the world. The
Romans loved to bathe. They learned how
to bring clean water from the country to
the city. Then they built public bath houses
in Rome. In time, they built the biggest
bath houses the world has ever seen.

From then on, every day became Bathing
Day in Rome. At one o'clock a signal was
given, telling people that the hot water was
ready. If a Roman wanted to bathe, he
went at once to the public baths. There he
paid his money and went inside.

He was not given a cake of soap, though.
The Romans did not have any bathing
soap. Instead, a bath attendant rubbed oil
into his skin. If the bather was *very* dirty,
sand was mixed into the oil. When the oily
mixture was rubbed off his skin, a lot of
dirt and sweat came off too.

The bath attendant also had a curved
metal tool called a "strigil" (*strij*-uhl). The
attendant used his strigil to scrape the oil,
sand, and dirt off the bather.

After that the attendant poured hot water over the bather. Then he poured cool water, and finally cold water. By the time the attendant had finished, the bather had taken something that was a little like our modern shower bath.

When the Roman bather was clean, he
put on fresh clothing and went into a much
larger room. He sat down and rested there,
and talked with his friends. Sometimes they
spent all afternoon at the public baths.
They certainly liked to bathe. But if the
Romans had used soap instead of sand,
oil, and a metal scraper, they might have
liked bathing even more.

In time, Rome was conquered by her enemies, and then the world changed very much. For hundreds of years, people lived in what are sometimes called the Dark Ages. Hardly anyone cared much about washing or keeping clean. Hardly anyone understood that it was important to bathe.

When the Dark Ages came to an end most people still remained very dirty. By then, men had forgotten how to bring clean water from the country to the city, as the Romans had. And it was difficult and expensive to heat water anyway.

Because they were dirty, people often got sick. But as yet there were no scientists or doctors who could tell people why they got sick, or how they could keep well.

During these times, the greatest kings and
queens hardly ever washed themselves. John
of England was a famous king. He may not
have been a very good one. And he
certainly couldn't have been a very clean
one. People said that he took a bath only
once every three weeks.

When King John did bathe, he used a
wooden tub. The tub was filled with hot
water. Then rose petals were dropped into
the water to make it smell sweet.

The king didn't use any soap, though. He
couldn't have used any, because no bathing
soap was made in England until long after
his rule was over.

More than three hundred years later, young Queen Elizabeth became the ruler of England. Elizabeth was a great queen. But she wasn't even as clean as King John had been. People who knew her said that she took a bath once every four weeks—whether she needed to or not!

At least by then a good deal of soap *was* being made in England, so perhaps the queen used some when she took a bath.

About four hundred years have passed since Queen Elizabeth sat on the English throne. Now we finally have begun to understand how important it is to keep clean and well-groomed.

Because we understand the importance of cleanliness, we have had to make certain changes.

We build our houses differently now. We run water pipes inside the walls. We also run water pipes under our streets, and build pumps to force the water through.

We have learned how to bring clean water from the country to the city, as the Romans did two thousand years ago. We also have learned how to heat water quickly and cheaply. Never before in history has it been quite as easy for so many people to keep clean and well-groomed.

By now scientists and doctors have
learned many facts about sickness and good
health. Today we know that germs are one
of the things that make us sick. But until
the first microscope was used, no one could
be sure that there really *were* any germs.

Under a microscope, something that
actually is very small appears to be very
big. When scientists began to use
microscopes they could see germs for the
first time. Then they could begin to study
germs and learn what they are like.

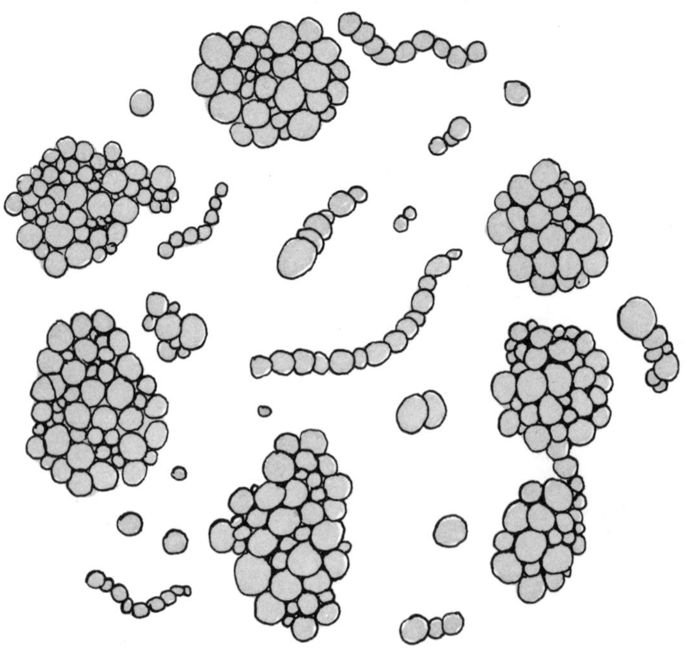

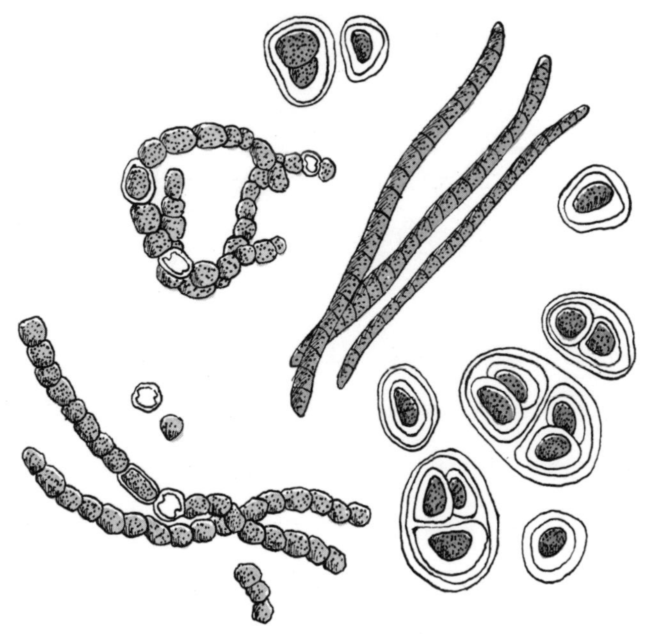

We know today that germs are living
things. They are very, very small.
Thousands of germs can live in a speck of
dirt. Thousands of germs can live in a drop
of water.

There are many different kinds of germs
in the world. Some kinds are not bad for
us. We can swallow them, and they won't
do us any harm. We can breathe them in,
through our nose or mouth, and they won't
do us any harm either.

But if other germs get inside our bodies,
they can make us very, very sick, indeed.

A virus is another living thing that can do us harm. A virus is even smaller than a germ.

Most viruses are so small that they cannot be seen under an ordinary microscope. But scientists have learned how to build and use a much stronger kind. It is called an electron microscope.

Scientists now can take pictures of different viruses by using an electron microscope. They can learn how viruses

live, and how to keep them from making
us sick.

Because doctors today know why we get
sick, they can help us to stay in better
health. They can give us rules to follow.
We will get sick a lot less often if we follow
their rules.

Doctors say that if we are able to, we
should take a bath or shower several times
a week. After running around and playing
for a long time, it's a wise idea to take a
shower if you can.

All good athletes know this. When
football or baseball players have finished
playing, they always take a shower. They
know that they must keep themselves clean,
to play their best, game after game, during
the championship season.

If you went into a football locker room
after a hard game, you would find most of
the players in the showers, lathering
themselves with soap.

The players make sure that they get rid
of all the dirt and sweat on their bodies.

They know that soap helps to loosen the
dirt, so that it will come off more easily.

After the players have rubbed themselves
all over with soap, they let warm water
wash the soap away. Both the sweat from
their skin and the dirt from the playing
field are carried away with the soapy lather.

When they take a shower, athletes always
make sure to wash the dirt off their feet.
And they remember to get the dirt out from
under their toenails. They have learned that
wherever there is dirt, there may be germs.

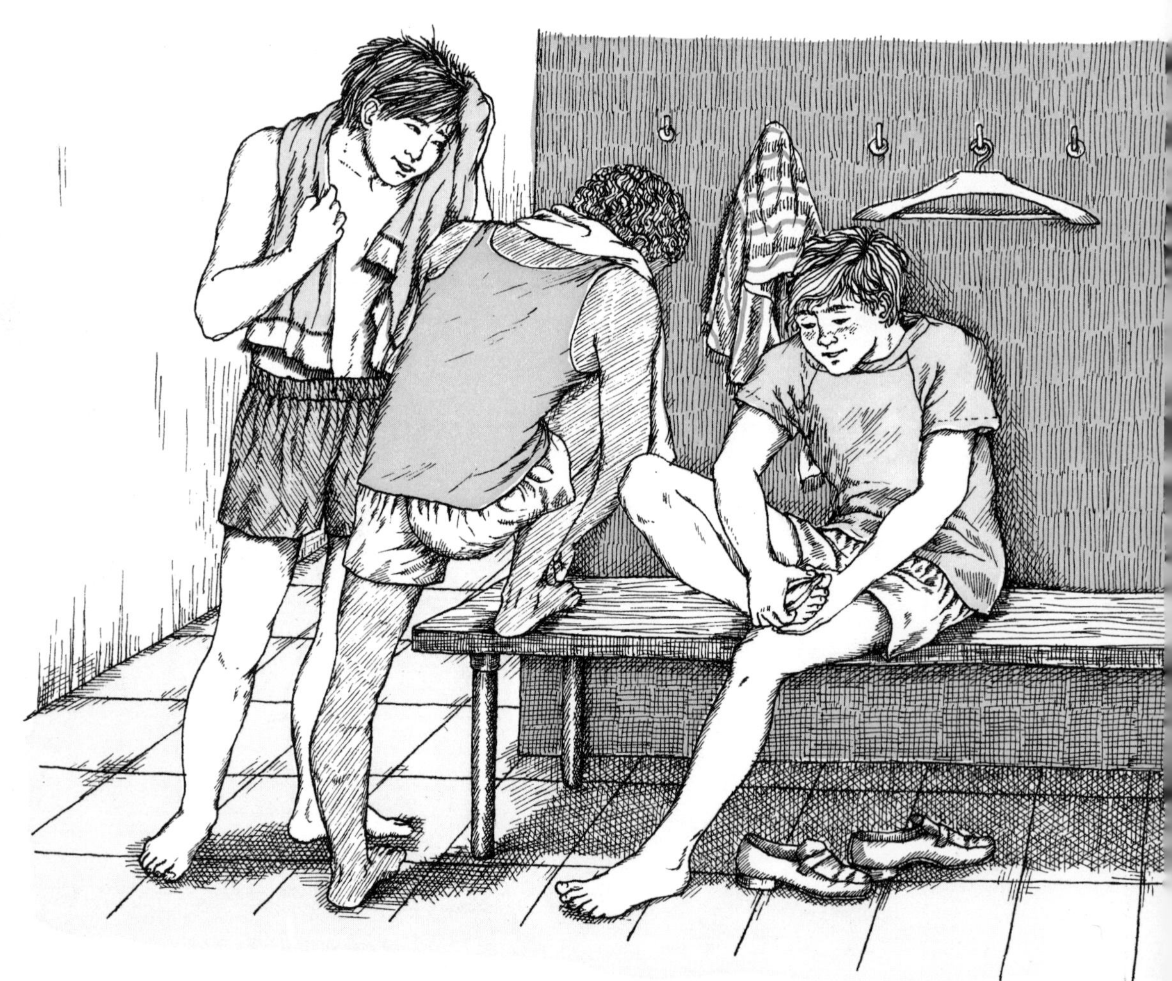

From time to time, they cut their toenails
too. This keeps their nails from growing too
long, and it makes it easier to keep
them clean.

Athletes always take good care of their
feet. They know that they can't hope to
play their best unless they can run fast.
And they can't run fast if their feet are
not in perfect condition.

Sometimes ball players wash their hair
while they're in the showers. But there's no
rule that says you have to do it this way.
You can wash your hair just as well in
a wash basin at home.

It's a good idea, though, to wash your
hair about once a week. Your mother can
tell you how often your hair needs washing.
She can help you if you find it too hard to
wash your hair by yourself.

And remember that your eyes will sting
if you get soap into them. So always keep
your eyes closed when your hair is being
washed.

Doctors tell us that the way we dress can be important to good health. When the weather is hot, we should wear less clothing than when it is cold. We don't want our bodies to get overheated or chilled.

If we go outside in winter weather, we must try to dress warmly enough to remain comfortable. When we come back inside, we must take off some of our clothes to keep our bodies from becoming too hot.

Wearing clean clothes also is important.
If we take a bath and then put on the same
dirty clothes, our bodies soon will be
covered with germs again.

So whenever possible, it's best to put on
clean underwear and socks, after a bath or
shower. Another good idea is to change our
underwear and socks each day, if we
possibly can.

Then, at night, we should hang up our
other clothing, to keep it neat, and to give
it a chance to air.

Some men find it hard to keep clean because of the work they do. Sometimes their wives have to take special care to get the dirt and grime out of their husbands' clothing.

Because they work on the land, farmers have a difficult time keeping clean. So do miners, who must work far underground. Men who operate machines often have a difficult time, too.

When they are at war, soldiers may have
the most difficult time of all. A soldier at
war doesn't live in a house with hot water
and a shower bath. Sometimes he must
sleep in the mud. If the fighting grows
heavy, he may not get a chance to bathe
for several days.

Years ago, soldiers in the field often got
sick. In most armies no one really knew how
to keep soldiers in good health.

But almost four hundred years ago, there was one small army where things were different. It was an army of knights who lived on Malta, an island near Africa, in the Mediterranean Sea.

The knights of Malta were special soldiers. They did have swords and armor, guns and cannons. They also had their own hospitals. When they weren't fighting, they took care of people who were sick. They were almost the only men of their time who understood the importance of soap and water. They knew that to stay well, people always must keep themselves as clean as they can.

The knights of Malta were brave fighters, too. But during the summer of the great siege, there weren't very many of them on the island. When their enemies, the Turks, came in their fleet of ships, they outnumbered the knights by four or five to one.

The knights held two fortresses on the
island. One was large and one was small.
As soon as the knights saw the Turks
coming, they shut themselves up inside the
two fortresses and prepared to fight.

Soon the siege began. At first the Turks fired their giant cannons at the small fortress. The shots tore great holes in the walls. After several weeks of terrible fighting, the small fortress fell to the enemy.

The rest of the knights fought on in the large fortress. Again and again the Turks fired their cannons. Again and again they attacked the walls. Each time they were thrown back after a terrible fight.

Then the enemy decided on a different plan. They began to dig a secret tunnel beneath the walls, in order to blow the walls up with gunpowder.

But the knights heard them digging. So they dug a tunnel of their own, caught the Turks by surprise, and drove them back to their camp, away from the walls.

All summer long the siege went on. The large fortress was almost in ruins. It seemed only a matter of days before the knights would have to give up the fortress and surrender.

But the outnumbered knights had two secret weapons. They knew how to care for cuts and wounds, so that in a short time most of their wounded soldiers could fight again. And they knew how to keep themselves clean, so that sickness never entered the fortress.

The Turks didn't bother about washing or keeping clean. As the summer days grew hotter, more and more of their soldiers got sick, until finally their army became too weak to fight its way into the fortress.

When the Turks saw that they had lost all hope of victory, they returned to their ships. They carried thousands of sick and wounded soldiers aboard. Then, as quickly as they could, they sailed for home.

From the walls of the fortress, the weary
knights watched them go. In triumph, they
raised their flag above the ruins. They had
won the great siege of Malta, one of the
most famous battles of history.

They had won it with guns and swords,
with daring and bravery. But they also had
won it with the soap and water that had
kept harmful germs from entering their lines
during the siege.

Today, doctors tell everyone to follow the same rules of cleanliness that the knights of Malta used during the great siege. They say that each morning and evening you should wash your face and neck with soap and water. When you do, you also should wash your ears, for they can get just as dirty as any other part of your skin.

A clean face, though, is not worth much, unless your hands also are clean. For good health, almost NOTHING is more important than having clean hands.

So, you should try to wash your hands each morning and evening. But that is only part of the job. You also should try to wash them before you eat. Most important of all, you MUST be SURE to wash your hands very well after each time you use the toilet.

During the day, many different germs
will collect on your hands. If you don't
wash them off, you will swallow some of
them with your food. Sooner or later, you
may swallow some germs that will make
you sick.

America's astronauts know how important

it is to have clean hands. While flying
through space, they wash after every meal.
They use "wet wipes"—small, damp pieces
of material, containing soap. "Wet wipes"
are made specially for the astronauts, to
keep them in good health as they soar
thousands and thousands of miles beyond
the earth.

There are several other things to
remember about your hands. One thing is
to keep your nails clean. The best way is to
use a soft nail brush, soap, and warm water.

But no one can have a nail brush always
handy. So you should try to keep a nail file
with you, and use it when your nails need
cleaning. You can carry the file in a case,
inside your pocket or purse.

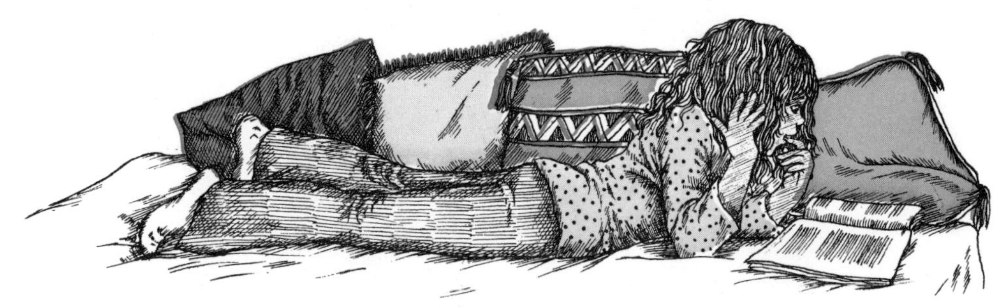

Another thing to remember is to keep your nails cut short. Don't bite them off, though. Do the job the right way, by trimming your nails neatly with a nail scissors. If you keep your nails cut short, you will make it that much harder for dirt—and harmful germs—to get under them.

After washing your face and hands, you should dry them off, to keep them from becoming chapped. The important thing is to dry your face and hands on something clean—on a paper towel or a cloth one.

During the famous siege, many of the knights of Malta were wounded in battle. They knew that if dirt got into their wounds, they would become sick. That is why, all during the hot summer, they took good care to keep their wounds clean.

Today, when people cut or scrape themselves, they know that it is important to keep germs out too. A cut or scrape is really like a small wound that a soldier might receive in battle.

Always treat small cuts and scrapes with care. Wash them out, as soon as you can, with soap and water.

After the water has dried, put a clean
bandage over the cut or scrape. In a few
days your skin will grow together, and the
cut or scrape will disappear.

Of course if you should ever hurt yourself
more seriously, tell your mother or father,

or one of your teachers at once. They will help you, and see to it that you are taken to a doctor or nurse without delay.

Even today, we still have many things to learn about germs and viruses. Doctors don't know yet which germ or virus causes the common cold. Until they do know, they won't be able to keep us from catching a cold now and then. But at least they can tell us how to treat a cold, once we have been unlucky enough to catch one.

The best thing to do when you catch a cold is to stay home and get enough rest. You should eat plain food and drink plenty of water. Grownups should not go to work, and children should not go to school while they have a cold.

By staying home, you will get over your cold much sooner. You also will do something else. You will *not* give your cold to your friends, or to other people you might meet on the way to school.

When you have a cold, there are millions of different germs inside your nose and throat. Each time you sneeze, many tiny droplets of moisture shoot out into the air. Thousands of germs are on each tiny droplet.

If other people breathe those droplets into their noses or mouths, they are very likely to catch your cold. To keep that from happening, you should cover your nose with a clean tissue before you sneeze. The tissue will trap the droplets of moisture, and prevent anyone else from catching your cold.

By using your tissue this way, you will
be helping to keep somebody else from
getting sick. You will be treating other
people with the same consideration that you
would like them to show toward you.

To enjoy good health, there is one other
part of your body that you must keep clean.
You can't do it with soap, though. That
part of your body is your teeth.

We are lucky today that we know how
to keep our teeth clean and healthy. A
hundred years ago it wasn't so easy to do.
There were no good dentists then to tell
people how to care for their teeth.

In earlier times, when a man wanted to clean his teeth, he wiped them off on a piece of cloth. Or he rubbed them with a piece of sponge, soaked in warm water. He probably didn't use a toothbrush, because very few were made until recently.

In earlier times, people didn't use toothpaste either. Instead, they tried to make their teeth white with a mixture of tobacco ashes and honey. Or they used charcoal, or the ground-up bones of a fish.

Most of the things they used didn't do very much good. Elizabeth, the famous Queen of England, had yellow teeth when she was a young woman. By the time she was old, her teeth had become black.

Because they had no dentists to help them, most kings and queens probably had very poor teeth. Maybe that's why they never smiled when an artist painted their picture. They knew that they would look better with their lips closed, their black or yellow teeth hidden from sight.

To have healthy teeth, there are a few simple things that you must do. The most important is to clean your teeth twice a day. The best times are after breakfast and after supper.

You also should try to brush your teeth in the right way. Dentists tell us that the upper teeth should always be brushed *down* from the gums. Lower teeth should always be brushed *up* from the gums. To finish the job, remember to brush the ends of your teeth too.

On their trips through space, America's astronauts always make it a point to keep their teeth clean. They take along a special spearmint-flavored toothpaste that can be swallowed without harm. They also take toothbrushes with them on their flights.

During one flight, a crew of astronauts sent back television pictures of a toothbrush floating around inside their space capsule. Millions of people saw the toothbrush, and knew that the astronauts were still brushing their teeth twice a day, even on a dangerous flight through space.

You can hurt your teeth, and break part of them off, by biting on something hard such as wood or metal. Don't chew pencils. And *never* be foolish enough to crack nuts with your teeth!

When you eat a piece of hard candy, don't chew it. Just let it dissolve in your mouth—and save your teeth.

There is one last rule that everyone should follow to keep in good health. Each night, be sure you get enough SLEEP.

If you do get enough sleep, you will become sick less often. Because of that, you will enjoy life a great deal more.

For when you are sick, you don't feel like working, or playing, or doing much of anything. But when you are well, you can go places, do things, and have fun.

INDEX